Janice VanCleave's
GRAVITY
Spectacular Science Projects

**FIND SCIENCE PROJECTS
@ YOUR LIBRARY**

The purchase of this book was made
possible by a Library Services and
Technology Act grant in conjunction
with the Connecticut State Library.
2004-2005

JANICE VANCLEAVE'S
SPECTACULAR SCIENCE PROJECTS

Animals
Gravity
Molecules

JANICE VANCLEAVE'S
SCIENCE FOR EVERY KID SERIES

Astronomy for Every Kid
Biology for Every Kid
Chemistry for Every Kid
Earth Science for Every Kid
Math for Every Kid
Physics for Every Kid

Janice VanCleave's
GRAVITY
Spectacular Science Projects

John Wiley & Sons, Inc.
New York · Chichester · Brisbane · Toronto · Singapore

In recognition of the importance of preserving what has been written, it is a policy of John Wiley & Sons, Inc. to have books of enduring value published in the United States printed on acid-free paper, and we exert our best efforts to that end.

Design and Production by BOOKMAKERS, LTD.
Illustrated by LAUREL AIELLO

The publisher and the author have made every reasonable effort to ensure that the experiments and activities in this book are safe when conducted as instructed but assume no responsibility for any damage caused or sustained while performing the experiments or activities in this book. Parents, guardians, and/or teachers should supervise young readers who undertake the experiments and activities in this book.

Library of Congress Cataloging-in-Publication Data

VanCleave, Janice Pratt
        [Gravity]
        Janice VanCleave's gravity.
                    p.   cm. -- (Spectacular science projects)
        Includes index
        ISBN 0-471-55050-7

Printed in the United States of America
10 9

CONTENTS

Dedicated to a special friend,
Holly Lynn Ruiz

Science is a search for answers. Science projects are good ways to learn more about science as you search for the answers to specific problems. This book will give you guidance and provide ideas, but you must do your part in the search by planning experiments, finding and recording information related to the problem, and organizing the data collected to find the answer to the problem. Sharing your findings by presenting your project at science fairs will be a rewarding experience if you have properly prepared the exhibit. Trying to assemble a project overnight results in frustration, and you cheat yourself out of the fun of being a science detective. Solving a scientific mystery, like solving a detective mystery, requires planning and the careful collecting of facts. The following sections provide suggestions for how to get started on this scientific quest. Start the project with curiosity and a desire to learn something new.

SELECT A TOPIC

The 20 topics in this book suggest many possible problems to solve. Each topic has one "cookbook" experiment—follow the recipe and the result is guaranteed. Approximate metric equivalents have been given after all English measurements. Try several or all of these easy experiments before choosing the topic you like best and want to know more about. Regardless of the problem you choose to solve, what you discover will make you more knowledgeable about gravity and how it affects you and your environment.

KEEP A JOURNAL

Purchase a bound notebook in which you will write everything relating to the project. This is your journal. It will contain your original ideas as well as ideas you get from books or from people like teachers and scientists. It will include descriptions of your experiments as well as diagrams, photographs, and written observations of all your results. Every entry should be as neat as possible and dated. Information from this journal can be used to write a report of your project, and you will want to display the journal with your completed project. A neat, orderly journal provides a complete and accurate record of your project from start to finish. It is also proof of the time you spent sleuthing out the answers to the scientific mystery you undertook to solve.

LET'S EXPLORE

This section of each chapter follows each of the 20 sample experiments and provides additional questions about the problem presented in the experiment. By making small changes to some part of the sample experiment, new results are achieved. Think about why these new results might have happened.

SHOW TIME!

You can use the pattern of the sample experiment to design your own experiments to solve the questions asked in "Let's Explore." Your own experiment should follow the sample experiment's format and include a single question about one thing, a list of necessary materials, a detailed step-by-step procedure, written results with diagrams, graphs, and charts if they seem helpful, and a conclusion answering and explaining the question. Include any information you found through research to clarify your answer. When you design your own experiments, make sure to get adult approval if supplies or procedures other than those given in this book are used. If you want to make a science fair project, study the information listed here and after each sample experiment in the book to develop your ideas into a real science fair exhibit. Use the suggestions that best apply to the project topic that you have chosen. Keep in mind that while your display represents all the work that you have done, it must tell the story of the project in such a way that it attracts and holds the interest of the viewer. So keep it simple. Do not try to cram all your information into one place. To have more space on the display and still exhibit all your work, keep some of the charts, graphs, pictures, and other materials in your journal instead of on the display board itself.

The actual size and shape of displays can be different, depending on the local science fair officials, so you will have to check the rules. Most exhibits are allowed to be 48 inches (122 cm) wide, 30 inches (76 cm) deep, and 108 inches (274 cm) high. These are maximum measurements and your display may be smaller than this. A three-sided backboard (see drawing) is usually the best way to display your work. Wooden panels can be hinged together, but you can also use sturdy cardboard pieces taped together to form a very inexpensive but presentable exhibit.

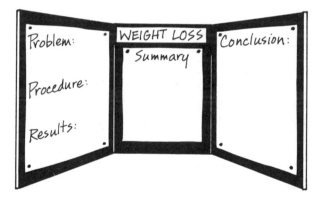

A good title of six words or less with a maximum of 50 characters should be placed at the top of the center panel. The title should capture the theme of the project but should not be the same as the problem statement. For example, if the question is "What is the effect of free-falling?" a good title for the project might be "Weight Loss." The title and other headings should be neat and large enough to be readable at a distance of about 3 feet (1 meter). You can glue letters on the backboard (you can use precut letters that you buy or letters that you cut out of construction paper), or you can stencil the letters for all the titles. A short summary paragraph of about 100 words to explain the scientific principles involved is good and can be printed under the title. A person who has no knowledge of the topic should be able to easily understand the basic idea of the project just from reading the summary.

There are no set rules about the position of the information on the display. However, it all needs to be well organized, with the title and summary paragraph as the main point at the top of the center panel and the remaining material placed neatly from left to right under specific headings. Choices of headings will depend on how you wish to display the information. Separate headings for Problem, Procedure, Results, and Conclusion may be used.

The judges give points for how clearly you are able to discuss the project and explain its purpose, procedure, results, and conclusion. The display should be organized so that it explains everything, but your ability to discuss your project and answer the questions of the judges convinces them that you did the work and understand what you have done. Practice a speech in front of friends, and invite them to ask you questions. If you do not know the answer to a question, never guess or make up an answer or just say, "I do not know." Instead, you can say that you did not discover that answer during your research and then offer other information that you found of interest about the project. Be proud of the project and approach the judges with enthusiasm about your work.

CHECK IT OUT!

Read about your topic in many books and magazines. You are more likely to have a successful project if you are well informed about the topic. For the topics in this book, some tips are provided about specific places to look for information. Record in your journal all the information you find, and include for each source the author's name, the name of the book, the numbers of the pages read, the publisher's name, where it was published, and the year of publication.

WHICH WAY IS DOWN?

PROBLEM

Do hanging objects always point in the same direction?

MATERIALS

scissors
ruler
string
paper clip
2 large books of equal
   height

PROCEDURE

1. Cut a 12-inch (30 cm) length of string.

2. Tie the paper clip to one end of the string.

3. Tie the free end of the string securely around the center of the ruler.

4. Stand the two books about 10 inches (25 cm) apart on a flat surface.

5. Support the ends of the ruler on the tops of the books.

6. Observe the position of the string and paper clip. To record the results, make a sketch or take a picture.

7. Hold one end of the ruler, and raise it about 4 inches (10 cm) above the top of the book.

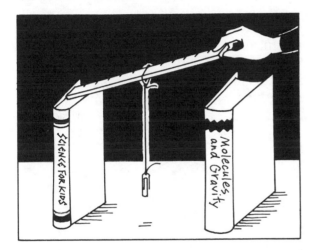

8. Again observe and record the position of the string and paper clip.

RESULTS

The paper clip pulls the string straight down, no matter how the ruler is positioned.

WHY?

The earth's gravity pulls the free-hanging paper clip straight down regardless of the position of the supporting ruler. **Gravity** is a force that pulls objects on or near the earth toward its surface. The direction of the pull is toward the center of the earth.

"Down" is always toward the earth's center. No matter what angle the surface is at, gravity pulls the object toward the center of the earth. Gravity is pulling all the yo-yos in the picture on page 5 toward the same spot, the center of the earth.

LET'S EXPLORE

1. Does the length of the string affect the direction of the hanging weight? Try the same experiment using different lengths of string. Record the string lengths and your results.

2. Would a heavier hanging object affect the results? How about a lighter object? Try the same experiment with different objects. Measure the weights of the objects used, if you have a scale; or use different numbers of the same object, for example, one, two, and then three paper clips.

3. Does the height of the end of the ruler change the direction of the weights? It was raised to 4 inches (10 cm). Would raising the ruler higher change the results? Measure the height of the ruler each time

it is changed and record the results. A protractor could be used to measure the angle of the ruler.

SHOW TIME!

1. A **plumb bob,** which is a hanging weight on a string, is used by carpenters to determine if a structure is vertical. The instrument is hung next to a structure and if the structure and the string are parallel, the structure is vertical. Try it yourself.

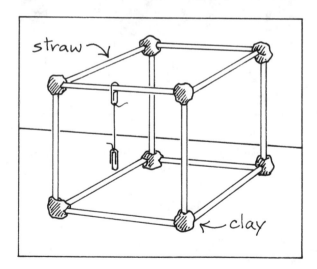

straw

clay

Construct an open box by connecting 12 drinking straws with balls of clay. Make a plumb bob by attaching one paper clip to each end of a 4-inch (10 cm) string. Open one of the paper clips, and hang it over a top supporting straw next to a vertical straw. Move the structure until the vertical straw next to the plumb bob is parallel with the hanging string. The structure is vertical when all the vertical straws are parallel with the hanging plumb bob.

2. Take a closer look at the world around you. How does gravity affect these situations?
- wire hanging between telephone poles
- necklaces and dangle earrings
- playground swing sets

A collection of pictures or drawings of these situations and others would make a good project display.

3. What causes the earth to have more gravity than its moon? A chart showing the amount of gravity on other planets would be interesting. A cartoon sketch could be drawn to show what beings might look like on different planets with varying pulls of gravity.

CHECK IT OUT!

Who is Sir Isaac Newton? A reference to his ideas about gravity should be included in your project report. Be sure to refer to him when giving your project presentation.

FREE-FALL

PROBLEM

Can the landing spot of free-falling objects, which are objects pulled only by gravity, be predicted?

MATERIALS

scissors
2 5-ounce (150 ml) paper
  cups
masking tape
yardstick (meterstick)
glass marble

PROCEDURE

1. Cut one cup down to a height of about 1 inch (2.5 cm).

2. Tape the short cup on one end of the stick.

3. Tape the taller cup to the stick about 4 inches (10 cm) away from the first cup.

4. Tape the other end of the yardstick (meterstick) to the door frame. The stick must be loose enough to be raised up and down easily.

5. Place the marble in the short cup.

6. Hold the stick with your fingers about 8 inches (20 cm) from the free end (just behind the taller cup).

7. Raise the cup end of the stick about 21 inches (53 cm) from the floor.

8. Allow the stick to fall to the floor. At the moment you release the stick, give it a gentle push downward. *Note: The gentle push is very important.* Repeat the experiment several times, each time changing the force of this push, until the following results are achieved.

RESULTS

The marble moves out of the short cup and falls into the taller cup. If the marble did not fall into the cup, adjust the downward force on the stick. Push a little harder if the marble falls short of the cup; decrease the force of the push if the marble moves past the taller cup.

WHY?

Gravity is a force that pulls objects on or near the earth's surface toward its center. Free-falling objects are pulled straight down toward the earth's center only by the force of gravity. The speed of the fall increases at a rate of 32 feet per second (9.8 m per sec) for every second of falling time. The push on the stick gives it a faster falling rate than the rate of free-falling objects. The faster-moving stick pulls the cup out from under the marble. The unsupported marble free-falls toward the floor. The path of the falling stick places the taller cup under the falling marble.

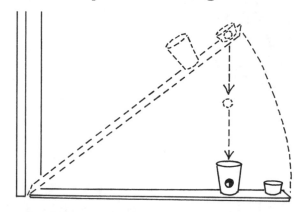

LET'S EXPLORE

1. Would a smaller or larger marble change the results? To discover the answer to this question, follow the procedure exactly, but use different-sized marbles. **Science Fair Hint:** The marbles, along with their individual results, could be used as part of a project display.

2. Does it matter how high the stick is raised before being released? Repeat the original experiment, raising the end of the measuring stick to different heights.

SHOW TIME!

1. What things are affected by gravity? A comparison of objects affected and not affected by gravity can be displayed. Use pictures of objects sitting on the earth's surface along with pictures of astronauts floating around in a spaceship.

2. The strength of the pull of gravity depends on the size of the object and its distance from the earth's surface. A way to display this would be a series of drawings of a ball and a boulder being pushed from the top of a mountain. Indicate that the two objects are falling side by side, with the final sketch showing the ball and the boulder hitting the surface: the ball disturbs the surface very little, but the boulder makes a large indentation.

3. An apple dropped into an imaginary hole cut through the earth, from one side to the other passing through the center, can be used to illustrate the pull of gravity toward the center of the earth. The diagram indicates that the apple's speed increases as it approaches the center. Does the apple stop at the center? Does the apple fall out of the hole? Get help from a teacher or parent in discovering the answer. For a project display, use

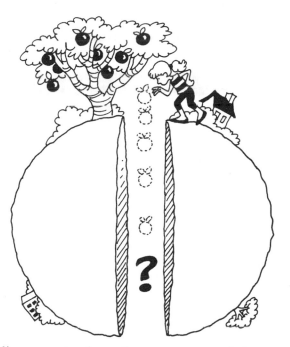

diagrams to show the movement of the apple.

CHECK IT OUT!

What does it mean to free-fall? Are all objects that fall through the air really free-falling? Use a science encyclopedia to discover the meaning of and examples of free-falling.

PAPER WEIGHT

PROBLEM

Does weight change the falling rate of objects?

MATERIALS

2 coins, 1 large and 1 small
typing paper
pencil
scissors

PROCEDURE

1. Lay the small coin on the paper and use the pencil to draw a complete circle around the edge of the coin.

2. Cut out the paper circle.

3. Hold the larger coin and the paper

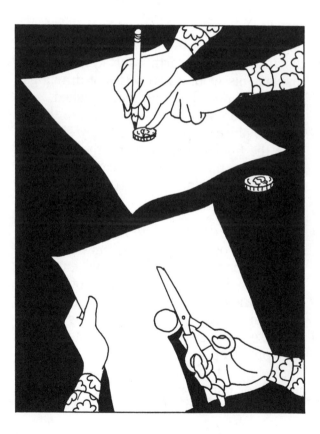

circle together, and raise them about 3 feet (1 m) above the floor.

4. Hold the pair so that the paper is under the coin and both are parallel with the floor. Be sure the paper does not extend past the edge of the coin.

5. Release and allow both coin and paper to fall at the same time.

6. Observe and record the position of the coin and paper as they fall.

7. Now reverse the position of the materials. Place the paper on top of the coin. Be sure the paper does not extend past the edge of the coin.

8. Raise the materials 3 feet (1 m) above the floor.

9. Hold the coin and paper parallel with the floor.

10. Release and allow the pair to fall to the floor.

11. Again observe and record the position of the coin and paper as they fall.

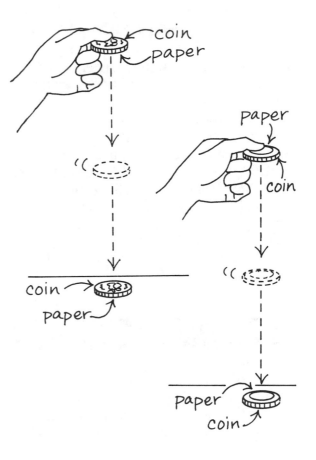

RESULTS

The coin and paper fall together regardless of their order. They separate only after hitting the floor.

WHY?

Because the acceleration of gravity is fixed, the lighter paper and the heavier coin both fall at the same rate. Gravity causes the speed of falling objects to increase at a rate of 32 feet per second (9.8 m per sec) for every second of falling time. The heavier coin pushes through the air with more force than does the lightweight paper circle, but because their falling rate is the same and they are positioned on top of each other, they move downward as if they were one object. Any separation of the pair upon striking the floor is the result of their bouncing on the surface.

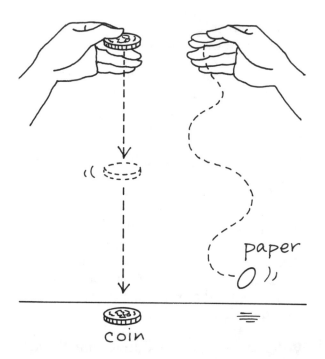

coin

paper

LET'S EXPLORE

1. Does the size of the paper affect the falling rate? Cut paper circles larger and smaller than a coin. Repeat the testing procedure and record the results for each separate circle of paper.

2. Is it the size of the paper or air resistance that changes the falling rate? Try dropping a coin and a paper circle separately, holding them side by side.

SHOW TIME!

1. Lay a ruler about 1 inch (2.5 cm) from the edge of a table and parallel to the edge. Place a coin and a paper clip next to each other on the table so that their inside edges touch the ruler. Hold the ruler and slide it so it pushes the clip and the coin toward the edge of the table. Ask a helper to observe the falling objects and to determine if they hit the floor at the same time. This experiment reduces the effect of air resistance while testing the effect of weight on the falling rate of objects.

2. While on the moon, an astronaut dropped a hammer and a feather from the same height. The two objects fell at the same rate. Would this happen on the earth? What causes any differences in dropping things on the moon and on the earth? Diagrams comparing the dropping of objects on the moon and the earth can be part of a project display.

3. Sky divers fall at a **terminal velocity** of about 120 miles per hour (192 km per hr). What is terminal velocity, and is it the same for all falling objects? What would cause parachutists, or some falling insects, to reach terminal velocity quickly? A project display could be a diagram using arrows to indicate the upward push of air on the falling object and the downward push of the object on air due to its weight.

4

LOCO-MOTION

Do objects with different horizontal speeds fall at the same rate?

MATERIALS

2 marbles, same size but
     different colors
ruler with groove down
     center
2 books

PROCEDURE

1. Place one marble near the edge of a table. For reference, this will be called marble B.

2. Position one end of a ruler on the table behind marble B, and the opposite end on the edge of one book.

3. Set the second marble, marble A, at the top of the ruler and release it.

4. Observe and record the movement of the marbles.

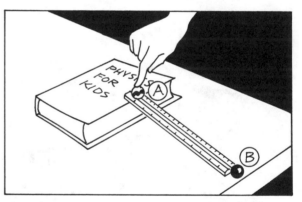

5. Now stack two books, and place the end of the ruler on the edge of the top book.

6. Position marbles A and B as before.

7. Release marble A, allowing it to roll down the elevated ruler.

16

8. Observe and record the movement of the marbles.

RESULTS

Marble A rolls down the ruler and strikes marble B. Both marbles move outward from the edge of the table, but marble B moves much farther than marble A. They appear to hit the floor at the same time. Raising the ruler changes only the distance that the marbles land from the edge of the table.

WHY?

Gravity pulls marble A down the inclined ruler. It increases in speed and energy as it rolls. Most of this energy is transferred to marble B upon collision, sending marble B outward from the edge of the table. Marble A continues to move forward after the two marbles collide, but at a slower speed than marble B. As soon as the marbles leave the table, gravity starts pulling them downward. They appear to strike the floor at the same time. Actually, marble B left the table a fraction of a second before marble A and hit the floor an equal fraction of a second before marble A. Even though the objects had different horizontal speeds, gravity pulled them downward at the same rate. Objects simultaneously thrown horizontally are the same height from the ground at any given moment during their fall.

LET'S EXPLORE

1. Would using a larger marble affect the results? Follow the same procedure, but use larger marbles. Make note of any changes in the movement of the marbles and the rate they fall.

2. Do the marbles have to be the same size? Use a large and a small marble. Vary the position of the marbles: Use the larger marble in position A, then reverse the positions, placing the smaller marble in position A.

SHOW TIME!

1. What causes the path of the marbles to be curved? Does this also cause the path of a thrown baseball to be curved?

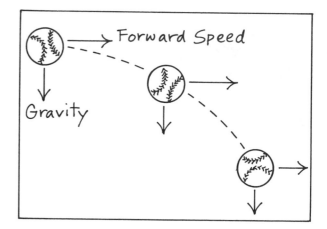

A diagram similar to the one showing the forces acting on a moving ball can be used as a project display.

2. Do free-falling objects and objects thrown horizontally fall at the same rate?

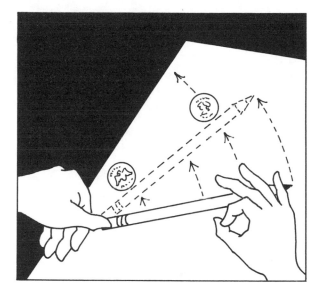

The diagram illustrates one way to test this. Two coins are placed so that as the pencil swings, it strikes both coins at the same time. The coin on the edge of the table will receive the least amount of force and should be tapped over the edge of the

table. The faster-moving end of the pencil propels the second coin outward from the table's edge. Observe and record the results of the falling coins.

3. Does gravity affect the forward speed of a bullet? Is gravity affected by the forward speed of the bullet? The answers to these questions will help you to answer this question: If one bullet is fired horizontally and a second bullet is dropped from the same height at the same time, will both bullets fall at the same rate and hit the ground at the same time? A diagram showing this could be used as part of the project display.

CHECK IT OUT!

Physics textbooks often have flash photographs of objects released simultaneously, one free-falling and the other projected horizontally. Check the sections on "projectiles" for this kind of photograph. Make an enlarged copy of this picture to use as proof that objects with a horizontal speed fall at the same rate as free-falling objects.

OFF TARGET

PROBLEM

What is the path of an object dropped from a moving body?

MATERIALS

1 cup (250 ml) rice, uncooked
sock
pencil

PROCEDURE

1. Pour the rice into the sock.

2. Tie a knot in the sock.

3. Lay the pencil on the ground to mark the target position.

4. Stand about 10 yards (10 m) from the target.

5. Hold the sock in your hand to the side of your body about waist high.

6. Run forward toward the target so that as you pass, the target will be to your side.

7. Drop the sock at the moment the sock is above the target.

8. Stop running as soon as the sock is released.

9. Observe and record the distance the sock lands from the target.

RESULTS

The sock lands on the ground past the target.

WHY?

Gravity starts pulling the sock down at the moment it is released, but the sock has the same forward horizontal speed as your

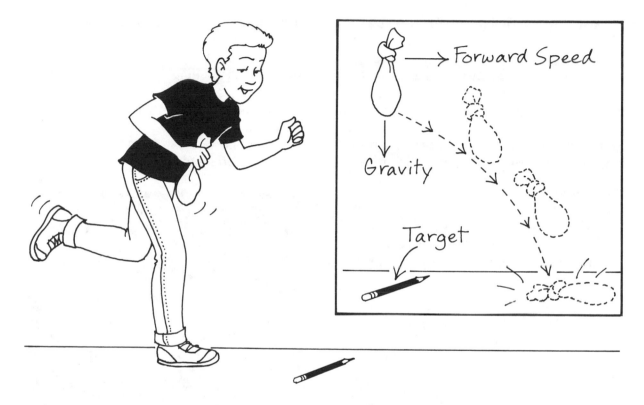

running speed. It continues to move forward, slowing due to air resistance, and at the same time is pulled downward by gravity until it strikes the ground at a point past the target. All objects with a constant horizontal speed accompanied by a downward increase in speed due to

gravity move forward in a curved path.

LET'S EXPLORE

1. What effect does the horizontal speed have on the landing spot of the sock?

Repeat the experiment twice: once at a slower running speed and once at a faster running speed. Record the distance the sock lands from the target area at the two speeds. **Science Fair Hint:** Pictures taken while performing the experiment make good displays. Always place a description of the part of the experiment that is being represented with the mounted picture.

2. What effect does the weight of the sock have on the path of the sock? Repeat the experiment twice, once with a heavier sock and once with a lighter sock. The weight of the sock can be varied by changing the amount of rice inside.

3. Does the height of the sock affect its landing spot? Repeat the experiment twice, once holding the sock higher than your waist and once holding the sock lower than your waist.

SHOW TIME!

1. What would be the path of objects projected upward from a moving vehicle? The drawing shows a spring toy sitting on a pencil box. Observe the distance and path the toy moves when the box is stationary and when the box is moving forward. Draw diagrams of the toy's path as it springs through the air. Keep records of any differences in distances that the toy moves when the speed of the box changes. The toy and box can be used as part of the project display.

2. What is a **projectile?** Give more than a definition of the term. Observe and discover examples of common projectiles such as a:
- bullet fired from a gun
- baseball thrown by a pitcher

- football passed by a quarterback
- rocket launched into space
- sky diver

Pictures of these and other projectiles, along with a sketch showing the path of each projectile, make a good project display.

CHECK IT OUT!

What does **trajectory** mean? Look up the definition and see if you can include it in your presentation.

LAUNCHER

6

PROBLEM

How are satellites launched into orbit around the earth?

MATERIALS

cardboard box
2 plastic rulers with groove
    down center
modeling clay
marble

PROCEDURE

1. Turn the cardboard box upside down on top of a table.

2. Place the edge of the box 10 inches (25 cm) from the edge of the table.

3. Lay one ruler on top of the box with 4 inches (10 cm) of the ruler extending over the edge of the box.

4. Hold the second ruler so that one end touches the end of the first ruler, with the grooves of the rulers lined up, and the second end is 2 inches (5 cm) above the box. Support that end by placing a piece of clay under it.

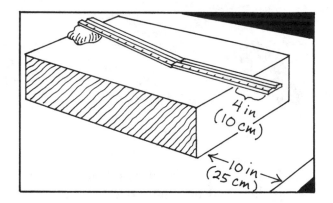

5. Position a marble at the top of the raised ruler, and then release the marble.

6. Observe the path of the marble.

RESULTS

The marble rolls down the ruler and off its end. The marble's path curves downward after it leaves the end of the "launcher" until it hits the floor.

WHY?

The table represents the earth, and the top of the box is a position above the earth's surface where the "marble satellite" is launched horizontally, parallel to the earth's surface. All satellites are raised to a desired height above the earth by booster rockets and then with additional rocket power the satellite is launched parallel to the earth's surface. Neither the "marble satellite" nor a space satellite continues to move forward in a straight line, because gravity pulls them toward the earth. The marble moves in a curved path out over the tabletop and past the edge of the table because gravity pulls it down and its launching speed pushes it forward. A space

satellite also moves in a curved path, but it continues to curve completely around the earth. Its path is then an entire circle, and it is said to be "in orbit" around the earth. The horizontal launching speed of any space satellite, like that of the marble, has to be great enough to balance the pull of gravity. Its forward speed, combined with the pull of gravity, keeps it away from the earth's surface and moving in a curved path.

LET'S EXPLORE

1. If the horizontal launching speed is too slow, gravity pulls the satellites back to

the earth's surface. Demonstrate this by repeating the experiment with the end of one ruler raised less than 2 inches (5 cm) above the box.

2. If the horizontal speed is too great, the craft breaks away from the earth's gravitational pull and escapes into space. You cannot cause the marble to actually escape into space, but repeating the experiment with the raised end of the launcher higher than 2 inches (5 cm) will demonstrate the movement of the satellite away from the normal path produced in the original experiment. **Science Fair**

Hint: The launcher and pictures of the launcher could be used as part of a project display.

3. Does the weight of the marble affect its speed? Follow the procedure of the experiment, but use a larger, heavier marble. Record any difference in the path of the marble.

SHOW TIME!

1. A cartoon diagram similar to the one shown may help to demonstrate the effect that launching speed has on placing satellites into orbit.

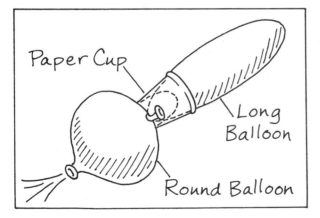

2. Multistaged rockets are used to place satellites into orbit. How is this achieved? What happens to each part of the system? Balloons and a paper cup can be used to demonstrate rocket staging. The diagram gives a clue to the construction of a multistage rocket system. A diagram of this balloon model along with pictures of actual multistaged rockets would make a good project display.

CHECK IT OUT!

1. Weather satellites stay in the same place above the earth's surface. They are said to be in a *geosynchronous orbit*. Read about geosynchronous orbits on pages 184 and 185 of *Astronomy for Every Kid* (New York: Wiley, 1991) by Janice VanCleave. Write to NASA for information about satellites. Your parent or teacher can assist you in securing the address.

2. Read about the space shuttle and how it launches satellites. What does it mean to say satellites "fall" into orbit? NASA can provide printed material about the space shuttle and satellites.

LET'S SWING

PROBLEM

What makes a pendulum swing?

MATERIAL

pencil
cardboard, 4 inches (10 cm)
   square
scissors
ruler
string
masking tape
book
washer

PROCEDURE

1. Draw a human figure on the cardboard square.

2. Cut the figure out with the scissors.

3. Cut a 1-yard (1 m) length of string.

4 in (10 cm)

4 in (10 cm)

4. Tape one end of the string to the end of the ruler.

5. Lay the ruler on a table, flat side down, with about 4 inches (10 cm) of the ruler extending over the edge of the table.

6. Place a book on the ruler to secure it to the table.

7. Tie the washer to the free end of the

string so that the washer hangs about 2 inches (5 cm) above the floor. Cut away any excess string.

8. Stand the cardboard figure so that it is facing the pendulum and is 8 inches (20 cm) away from the hanging washer. Tape the figure to the floor.

9. Holding the washer between your thumb and index finger, move the washer until it is in front of but not touching the cardboard figure's face.

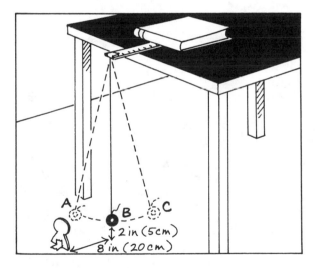

10. Release the washer, and allow it to freely swing. Do not push it.

RESULTS
The washer swings back and forth, but it does not strike the cardboard figure.

WHY?
The washer on the string is a pendulum. At position A, the washer is pulled down by gravity. The speed of the moving pendulum increases until it reaches the vertical position at point B. The pendulum begins to move upward at point B. As it moves upward, gravity continues to pull down on the washer, resulting in a decrease in speed until it stops at point C. When the pendulum stops moving upward, gravity takes over and pulls the weight down again, starting the swing in the opposite direction. The cardboard figure is never struck because the height of each swing decreases with each sweeping motion until finally the pendulum stops.

LET'S EXPLORE

1. Does amplitude (the height the pendulum is raised to the side) affect the swing? Repeat the experiment, pulling the weight to different heights to determine if the swing is affected.

2. Would the pendulum swing farther if a heavier weight was used? Increase the number of washers on the string, and repeat the experiment. Record the results observed for each number of washers used. Other things to look for when you change the number of washers (thus, the weight) are:

- Whether a different weight changes the speed of the swing. To find out, count the number of swings in 10 seconds for each of the different weights.
- Whether weight affects the length of time the pendulum swings before stopping.

3. Does the length of the string affect the swing? Use different lengths of string. Pull the weight to the same amplitude each time so the results of each length of string can be compared.

SHOW TIME!

1. What causes the pendulum to stop swinging? How does the gravity on the earth compare to the gravity on the moon?

Would a pendulum swing the same length of time on the moon as it would on the earth? One way to explain your answer

moon. Compare the speed of the swinging children and the duration of their swinging. A diagram similar to the one shown could be used to accompany your explanation.

2. Would a pendulum clock keep correct time on the moon? Would the time on the clock be slower, faster, or the same as on the earth? Diagrams showing the faces of pendulum clocks on the earth and on the moon could be used as a project display. Get help from a teacher or parent in calculating any time differences.

CHECK IT OUT!

1. Read about pendulum clocks and discover why the pendulum continues to swing and the purpose of the pendulum.

2. Galileo has been credited with discovering the relationship between the length of a pendulum and the time of its swing. Find the story that explains how he discovered this relationship. A diagram representing this story can enhance your project display, or you could use it in an oral presentation.

would be to show two children of equal weight swinging in comparable swings, one on the earth and the other on the

8

OFF BALANCE

Why do things fall over?

MATERIALS

ruler
marking pen
empty cardboard pencil
   box—or a box about 2 ×
   5 × 9 inches (5 × 13 ×
   23 cm)
scissors
string
washer
push pin
book
modeling clay

PROCEDURE

1. Use the ruler and marking pen to draw an X across one of the largest faces of the box.

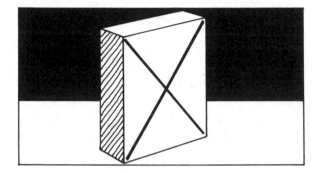

2. Cut a 12-inch (30 cm) length of string.

3. Tie a washer to one end of the string.

4. Insert the push pin in the center of the X on the box.

5. Tie the free end of the string around the push pin.

6. Lay the book on the edge of a table.

7. Set the box on the book so that the washer hangs freely over the edge of the table.

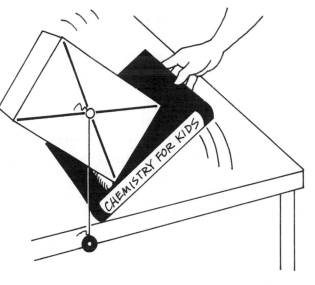

8. Press a small roll of clay on the book in front of the box.

9. Slowly raise the end of the book that is away from the clay. The clay should keep the box from sliding down the book.

10. Continue to slowly raise the book until the box topples over.

RESULTS

The string moves toward the corner of the box as the box is being raised. When the string passes the corner, the box falls over.

WHY?

The **center of gravity** is the point at which the weight of an object appears to be located. The push pin on the outside of the box points to the box's center-of-gravity position inside the box. The hanging string shows the direction in which the weight of the box is being pulled. Tilting the book changes the position of the box, but the string continues to point straight down. The box sits flat on the book as long as its weight is directed down through the bottom of the box (as indicated by the string); but when the string passes the corner of the box, it indicates that the weight of the box is pulling the box forward and it topples over.

LET'S EXPLORE

1. Does the height of an object affect the angle at which it can lean before falling over? Repeat the experiment using boxes of different heights. Measure the height that each box can be raised before it topples over. **Science Fair Hint:** Make drawings showing the difference in the heights of the boxes and the angle at which each falls over. The diagrams can be displayed as part of a project.

2. Would a wider base affect the amount of the tilting angle necessary to cause the box to fall? Use a box with a wider base. Record the angle at which each box falls over. **Science Fair Hint:** Make diagrams of each design used and keep the constructed boxes as part of your project display.

SHOW TIME!

1. Does the length of your feet affect how far you can lean before falling? Stand with your heels against a wall. Lean as far forward as possible without falling. Try wearing a much longer pair of shoes. Can you lean farther? Photographs with explanations of results make great project displays.

2. Observe the world around you to discover how the shapes of objects affect their stability. Photographs or drawings can be used along with a description of why an object will or will not easily topple fall over. How is this stability achieved? Make sketches to illustrate how toys and furniture can be made to be more stable.

CHECK IT OUT!

Why has the famous Leaning Tower of Pisa not toppled over? Discover why it leans. How much does it tilt each year? When will it fall? What suggestions have been made by engineers to stop any further leaning?

over. Some suggestions for study are:
- shapes of people. What body structure would make a person less likely to fall over?
- stability of toys and children's furniture. Information about center of gravity is used by engineers in designing toys and furniture for children. Toys and children's furniture are usually more stable, less likely to

BALANCING POINT

9

PROBLEM

Can an object's center of gravity (its point of balance) be changed?

MATERIALS

typing paper
pencil with a flat eraser
scissors
construction paper (any
    color)
modeling clay
small paper clips

PROCEDURE

1. Lay the typing paper over the diagram of the bee pattern.

2. Use a pencil to trace the bee on the

typing paper. Then cut out the bee design with the scissors.

3. Use the paper bee as a stencil to draw the design on the construction paper.

4. Cut out the bee from the construction paper.

5. Press a piece of clay on a table. Stand the pencil, eraser pointing up, in the clay.

6. Place the bee on top of the pencil's eraser. Move the bee to find the point where the bee balances.

7. Attach one paper clip to each wing tip. Adjust the clips so that the bee balances on the tip of its head.

RESULTS

Without the paper clips, the bee balances on a point near the center of its body. The bee balances on the tip of its head when the paper clips are added.

WHY?

The place on the bee where it can be balanced is called the **center of gravity.** This is the point where all the parts of the bee exactly balance each other. All objects can be balanced and thus have a center of

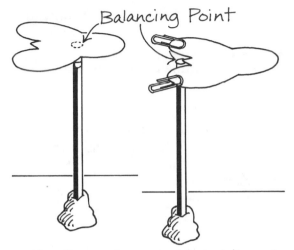

Balancing Point

gravity. Supporting any object at its center-of-gravity position will make it balance. Adding the paper clips increases the weight on the wings. Weight is a measure of the forces of gravity, a downward pull on an object. The weight of the metal clips shifts the position of the center of gravity to the head of the bee.

LET'S EXPLORE

1. Could the paper clips be positioned so that the center of gravity is on the tip of one of the wings or at the tail of the bee?

2. Try using thicker paper or cardboard to make the bee. More paper clips will be required to balance the bee on its head. Does it make a difference if the clips are attached to the wings or all dangled from one clip as a chain?

3. Is the shape of the bee important? Could a bee balance on its head if these changes in structure are made?
- longer wings
- shorter wings
- wings of different lengths
- longer body
- shorter body

Science Fair Hint: Keep a record of your results. Samples of the different-shaped bees constructed and a summary of the results can be used as part of a project display.

SHOW TIME!

1. The diagram gives another example of moving weights around to make an object balance on a specific point. Arrange a ruler, string, pencil, and ball of clay so that the ruler balances on the edge of a table as in the drawing. Experiment to determine the best length of string to use and the amount of clay needed. Other things to explore are: How close can you get the center of gravity to the end of the ruler? What changes would be needed to balance a yardstick (meterstick)? Display the materials and photographs taken of the positions of the materials.

2. A cardboard tightrope walker can be used to further study the effect of adding weights in order to position the center of gravity at a certain point. Start with a

4-inch (10 cm) square of corrugated cardboard to make the figure shown in the drawing. Insert a piece of wire about 12 inches (30 cm) long through the cardboard to form long armlike structures. Use 18- to 20-gauge wire (the wire needs to be flexible, but stiff enough to hold weight on the tips). The wire simulates the balancing pole used by circus tightrope walkers. Experiment with different weights on the tightrope walker's arms. You can design separate experiments to find the answers to these questions:

- Is it easier for a tall or short tightrope walker to balance on the wire?
- Which helps most, a short or long balancing pole?

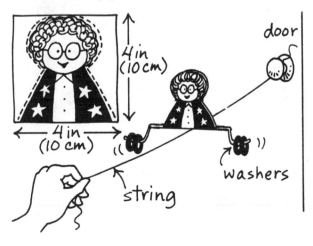

- Where is the best place to hold the balancing pole?

3. Natural bridges provide great examples of how the center of gravity of a structure can keep large rocks and heavy sections of land suspended. Make drawings or collect pictures of examples of this natural phenomenon of balancing points. You may try to build your own examples of a natural bridge as a display using ice cream sticks. The diagram gives a clue to the

structure. Use your own designs and try different materials. Take pictures of each structure and use one of the more stable bridges as part of the project display.

CHECK IT OUT!

When will a seesaw balance? Read about the law of moments in a physical science book, and learn to predict where each person must sit in order to balance a seesaw.

SPRINGY

PROBLEM

How does a spring scale work?

MATERIALS
masking tape
plastic Slinky™
pencil
5-ounce (150 ml) paper cup
scissors
ruler
string
typing paper
index card
marking pen
4 identical coins

PROCEDURE

1. Tape the end of the Slinky to the top of a door frame. The Slinky needs to hang

freely and about ¼ inch (0.6 cm) away from the vertical frame.

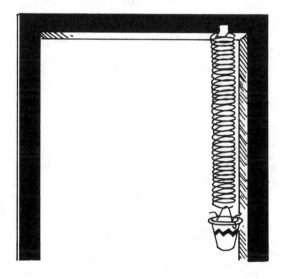

2. Use a pencil to punch holes on opposite sides of the cup under the rim.

3. Cut an 8-inch (20 cm) length of string.

4. Tie the ends of the string through each hole in the cup.

5. Loop the string on the bottom turn of the hanging Slinky.

6. Tape a sheet of typing paper to the inside door frame behind the cup.

7. To make a pointer, cut a $2 \times \frac{1}{4}$-inch (5×0.6 cm) strip from an index card. Tape this paper pointer under the rim of the cup so that it points toward the paper.

8. Use the marker to mark the position of the paper pointer on the typing paper. Label the mark "0."

9. Place one coin in the cup. Mark the position of the pointer on the paper and label the mark "1."

10. Continue to add coins one at a time to the cup. Mark and label each position of the pointer on the paper with the number of coins in the cup.

11. Observe the distance between the marks.

RESULTS

The cup moves downward as coins are added. Each additional coin moves the cup the same distance.

WHY?

A **spring scale** is an instrument used to measure the weight of an object. On earth, **weight** is the name used for the measure of the force of attraction between an object and the earth. This force is called **gravitational attraction.** The weight of the coins would change if measured on another celestial body that had a gravitational force different from that of the earth. The coins would weigh less on the moon than on the earth because the moon's force of gravity is less than that of the earth. The amount of weight depends on the **mass** (the amount of matter present). Unlike weight, the mass of the coins would not change no matter where they were taken. They would have the same mass on the moon as on the earth because mass is a measure of the amount of particles present. You would weigh less on the moon than on the earth, but your size would not change because your body mass (all the molecules that make up your body) would not change. You gain weight when more particles (mass) are added to your body just as adding more coins to the cup increases the total mass of the coins and thus increases the weight. Since the coins are of equal mass, two coins have twice as much weight as one coin. Two coins move the cup down twice the distance that one coin does. Each additional coin moves the cup a predictable distance—four coins should move the cup a distance four times that of one coin.

LET'S EXPLORE

1. Would the coins move a metal Slinky the same distance? Repeat the experiment using a metal Slinky.

2. Would different coins affect the distance the Slinky moves? Repeat the experiment using four heavier coins.

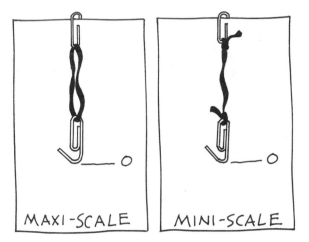

MAXI-SCALE   MINI-SCALE

SHOW TIME!

1. Assemble the cardboard pieces, paper clips, and rubber bands as shown in the diagrams to construct two hand-held scales. Add weights such as paper clips or washers to the bottom hook to determine the distance the scale moves with each number of weights. Mark the position of the bottom of the metal hook after each weight is added. These scales can be used as project displays to show the difference in the construction of scales used to measure small and large weights.

2. Does weight vary with location? Do objects weigh less at different points on the earth? Do people weigh less in an airplane at 30,000 feet (9,144 m) than on the earth's surface? Would there be a change in the weight of objects at the bottom of a mine shaft? Discover the changes in the pull of gravity at various distances from the earth's surface. Use

these values to make a diagram of an astronaut at different distances from the earth's surface.

CHECK IT OUT!

Measuring is an important part of an experimenter's work. Read about the various types of weighing instruments. Discover which instruments are affected by changes in gravity. Display pictures showing the changes in scales through the years.

ON THE MARK

PROBLEM

How is a balance used to measure mass (the amount of matter present)?

MATERIALS

pencil
2 5-ounce (150 ml) paper cups
scissors
ruler
string
wire clothes hanger with
   cardboard tube
door with door knob
index card
masking tape
1 sheet of typing paper
penny
small paper clips

PROCEDURE

1. Use a pencil to punch holes on opposite sides of each cup under the rim.

2. Cut two 8-inch (20 cm) lengths of string.

3. Tie the ends of one string through the holes in one of the cups. Repeat for the other cup.

4. Remove the cardboard tube from the wire hanger.

5. Hook the wire hanger on a door knob.

6. Cut a $2 \times \frac{1}{4}$-inch (5×0.6 cm) strip from an index card. Cut one end of the strip to a point.

7. Tape the paper pointer in the center of the wire hanger.

8. Tape a sheet of paper behind the hanger. Draw a line below the paper pointer. This will be referred to as the balance mark.

9. Place the penny in the cup on the right.

10. Observe the position of the pointer.

11. Add paper clips, one by one, to the other cup until the pointer returns to the balance mark.

RESULTS

The pointer moves off the balance mark when the penny is put in the cup. The addition of each paper clip moves the pointer closer to the balance mark until finally the pointer indicates that the cups are balanced by pointing at the balance mark.

WHY?

A **balance** is an instrument that compares the masses of two objects. The mass of the coin placed in the right cup is equal to the mass of the paper clips in the left cup. The exact mass of an object can be determined by comparing it with a known mass. The unknown mass is placed on one side and known masses are added to the opposite side until the instrument balances. When the instrument is balanced, the unknown mass equals the sum of the known masses.

LET'S EXPLORE

Can you determine the exact mass of various objects? Ask a pharmacist to measure the mass of one paper clip. Repeat the experiment using the known mass of the paper clip to determine the mass of different objects: pencil, ring, 1 teaspoon (5 ml) of sugar, ¼ cup (60 ml) of water.

SHOW TIME!

You can construct balances to measure large and small items. The ruler balance in the diagram below can be used to compare the masses of equal cupfuls of materials such as sand, sugar, water, or pebbles. Display the balance along with cupfuls of the materials measured properly arranged in order of their mass. The straw balance

in the diagram on page 47 is a more sensitive balance that you can make. Place a fly or other insect on one of the pans, and use paper circles as a **counterweight** (the weight on the opposite side of the balance from your object). The actual mass

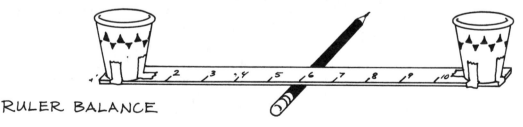

RULER BALANCE

STRAW BALANCE

of the paper circles could be determined on a pharmacist's scale, and this mass can be used to determine the mass of the fly and other lightweight materials. Display the balance as part of the science project. The insect, with a label stating its mass, can be mounted or placed in an empty see-through pill bottle.

CHECK IT OUT!

1. Would a change in gravity affect the measurements on a balance? How would a balance behave in an orbiting spacecraft? Read about weight-measuring instruments, and discover if balances are affected by gravity changes.

2. "Inertia balances" can be used in a "weightless" environment. How does an inertia balance measure mass? Most physics books describe this instrument. For a simple explanation and instructions for making an inertia balance, see the experiment called "Space Balance," page 170 in *Astronomy for Every Kid* (New York: Wiley, 1991) by Janice VanCleave.

UP OR DOWN

12

PROBLEM

Does gravity have an effect on plant growth?

MATERIALS

6 pinto beans
small jar with straight sides
water
refrigerator
paper towels
8 × 12-inch (20 × 30 cm)
    sheet of aluminum foil
marker

PROCEDURE

1. Place the beans in a jar.

2. Cover the beans with water, and store the jar in a refrigerator overnight.

3. After 24 hours, pour the water out of the jar, and empty the beans onto a paper towel that is folded in half.

4. Roll the towel around the beans.

5. Place the paper-towel roll containing the beans in the center of the aluminum foil, and moisten the paper towel with water.

6. Fold the aluminum foil around the paper roll. Secure the ends of the foil by bending them over.

7. Use the marker to draw an arrow on the aluminum. Point the arrow to one end of the aluminum roll.

8. Stand the roll in an empty jar with the arrow pointing up.

9. Allow the roll of beans to stand undisturbed for five days. Then carefully open the package so as not to disturb the beans.

10. Observe and make diagrams to record the growth of the beans.

11. Moisten the paper roll with water as before.

12. Roll the package around the beans as before.

13. Place the roll in the jar with the arrow pointing **down.**

14. After another five days, open the package. Observe again and make drawings to record the growth of the beans.

RESULTS

After five days, the bean sprout roots grow down and the stems grow upward. Turning the roll upside down results in the roots and stems making a 180-degree turn so that again the roots grow down and the stems grow up.

WHY?

Geotropism is the movement of a plant due to the pull of gravity. This movement is the result of the position of a growth hormone called **auxin** in the plant. Gravity

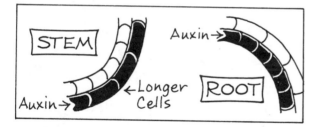

pulls the chemical downward, causing it to collect in the lower part of the plant. In a stem, the cells grow longer on the side where there is more auxin, causing the stem to bend upward. Root cells grow longer on the side where there is a smaller amount of auxin, causing the root to bend

downward. The diagram shows the position of the auxin and the direction of the growth produced in stem and root cells. One of the reasons that roots may wander around in erratic patterns is that the auxin moves down the root due to gravity. This causes cell growth on one side of the root, and thus the root changes directions.

LET'S EXPLORE

1. Do roots always grow down and stems up? Repeat the experiment, standing the roll of beans at different angles. **Science Fair Hint:** Display diagrams showing the results of each experiment.

2. How would plants grow in a rotating space station? Try this experiment using a stereo turntable. A rotating turntable produces a simulated field of gravity with an outward force that affects roots and stems. Prepare rolls of beans using paper towels and aluminum foil as in the experiment. Leave the rolls undisturbed for three days; then place them opposite each other on the turntable. Set on the fastest speed and allow the machine to rotate

continuously for three days. Open the packages, and observe the direction of the stem and root growth. **Science Fair Hint:** Display the record player, and use photographs of the results of the stem and root growth. Use this experiment and information from other sources to prepare an explanation of how plants might grow in space. For more information about artificial gravity, see an experiment called "Fake," page 198 in *Astronomy for Every Kid,* (New York: Wiley, 1991) by Janice VanCleave.

SHOW TIME

How long does it take gravity to make a change in the direction of a plant's growth? Design different ways to position plants so that the stem and roots bend due to the effects of gravity. Be sure that the plants are in an area of equal lighting to prevent the plant from changing directions due to a light source. When experimenting, scientists must try to test only one phenomenon at a time. Display plants used.

G-FORCES

13

PROBLEM

What causes a feeling of weightlessness?

MATERIALS

scissors
ruler
construction paper, any
   bright color
cellophane tape
string
2-liter soda bottle

PROCEDURE

1. Cut a 2 × 8-inch (5 × 20 cm) strip from the paper.

2. Fold the paper strip in half four times and tape the edges together.

3. Cut a 12-inch (30 cm) length of string.

4. Tie one end of the string around the center of the folded paper.

5. Hold the free end of the string, and insert the folded paper into the plastic soda bottle.

6. Pull up on the string until the bottle is about 2 inches (5 cm) above the table.

7. Release the string.

8. Observe the movement of the bottle and the folded paper.

RESULTS

When the string is released, the bottle and the paper fall. The paper hangs at the top of the bottle until the bottle stops, and then the paper falls to the bottom of the bottle.

attraction between two objects is called a **G-force**. A G-force of one is produced by the earth's gravity, 32 feet per second per second (9.8 m per sec per sec). True free-falling would occur in a **vacuum** (a space entirely empty) where not even gas particles press against the falling object. Even with the collision with air particles, all falling objects experience a feeling of zero gravity (apparent weightlessness). The paper and the bottle are falling at the same speed with only air molecules pushing against them. As long as both are falling through the air, like astronauts in a spacecraft orbiting the earth, there is an apparent weightlessness. Both the spacecraft with the astronauts and the bottle with the paper experience a feeling of zero gravity (weightlessness) as long as they are falling together.

LET'S EXPLORE

1. Would the length of the string affect the experiment? Repeat the experiment using different string lengths. Record the string lengths and your results.

WHY?

Objects falling toward the earth are said to be **free-falling** if the only thing pulling or pushing on them is gravity. The force of

2. Does the height the bottle falls from affect the results? Repeat the experiment raising the bottle to various heights greater than 2 inches (5 cm). Record the heights and your results.

SHOW TIME!

1. Stand on a bathroom scale in an elevator to actually measure apparent changes in the force of gravity (G-forces). What happens to the scale reading as the elevator moves up and down? You are not changing in size as the elevator moves, so what causes the changes in the readings? Photographs of you in the elevator can be used as part of your project display. Display the results of the scale readings with explanations of their differences.

2. Measure the G-forces on a roller coaster ride at an amusement park with a homemade accelerometer (an instrument used to measure the pull of gravity). Construct the accelerometer by assembling a 6-inch-square (15-cm square) piece of

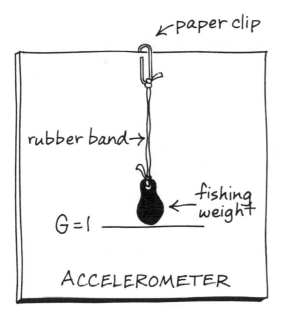

paper clip

rubber band→

G = 1

fishing weight

ACCELEROMETER

1" mark and greater than 1 when the weight moves below the "G = 1" mark. Determine what part of the ride produces G-forces greater or less than 1. Use the accelerometer and diagrams indicating G-forces at different parts of the ride as part of a project display.

cardboard, a rubber band, a paper clip, and a fishing weight as shown in the diagram. The weight must be heavy enough to stretch the rubber band so that the weight hangs in the center of the cardboard. Mark the bottom position of the hanging weight and label the mark "G = 1." Observe the accelerometer as you ride the roller coaster. The G-force is less than 1 when the weight moves above the "G =

CHECK IT OUT!

1. Is there a place of zero gravity? At what distance from the earth's surface are spacecraft no longer pulled toward the earth? Is this where zero gravity exists? You could include this information when giving a project presentation.

2. Collect pictures from magazines or take photographs of situations that represent weightlessness. Two examples of situations that produce weightlessness (if only for a split second) would be a girl jumping on a pogo stick and a boy bouncing on a trampoline, both at the very top of the jump or bounce just before they start falling back to the earth.

PADDLE WHEEL

PROBLEM

Does the mass of falling water affect the energy it produces as it falls?

MATERIALS

scissors
ruler
index card
glue
large, empty thread spool
pencil
water from a faucet

PROCEDURE

1. Cut six separate 1-inch (2.5 cm) squares from an index card.

2. Bend about ⅛ inch (0.3 cm) of one edge down on each square.

3. Glue the bent edges to the side of the thread spool. Evenly space the paper squares around the spool to form paddles.

4. Allow the glue on the paddles to dry completely.

5. Push a pencil through the center hole of the spool. The pencil must be thin enough

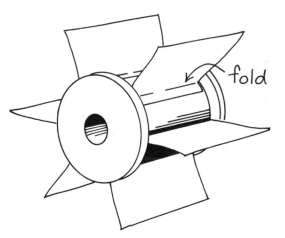

to allow the spool to spin around freely.

6. Turn a faucet on slightly, allowing a very small, steady stream of water to flow out.

7. Hold the ends of the pencil, and place the spool so that the paper paddles are about 2 inches (5 cm) under the faucet in the stream of water.

8. Observe the speed at which the spool turns.

9. Increase the flow of water and again place the paddles under the stream.

10. Again observe the speed at which the spool turns.

11. Record any differences in the turning speeds of the spool when placed in different amounts of falling water.

RESULTS

The spool spins faster when placed under a larger amount of falling water.

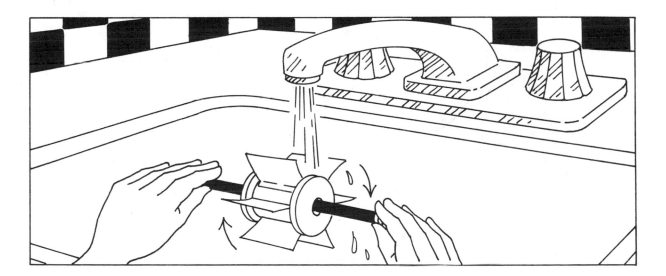

WHY?

The energy of any falling material depends on the distance it falls, the pull of gravity, and the material's mass (the amount of the material present). The energy of the falling water was transferred to the paddle, forcing it downward. As each paddle moved down, it turned the spool and thus placed another paddle under the stream of water. This continued, causing the spool to spin. As the amount of water increased, the mass hitting each paper paddle

SALT

increased, and the spool turned faster. **"Gravitational potential energy"** is possessed by things that can fall (anything raised off the ground). This energy increases with the height and mass of the object.

LET'S EXPLORE

1. Would the distance that the water fell affect its energy? Use a slow stream of water. Hold the ends of the pencil, and place the spool so that the paper paddles are in the stream of water. Move the spool up and down in the stream, and observe any differences in the turning speed of the spool. **Science Fair Hint:** You could measure the distance from the faucet and count the number of turns in a 5-second time period. This gives recorded data to display. Photographs of the spool being held in the stream of water can also be used as part of a project display.

2. Does it matter if the falling water is fresh or salty? To be able to compare the same amounts of water, use a paper cup with a hole in the bottom instead of the faucet as in the diagram. Ask a helper to keep the cup full.

SHOW TIME!

1. How is gravitational potential energy of falling water used to make electrical energy? A model or diagram can be displayed. An explanation of the change from one form of energy to the other would make an interesting oral presentation.

2. Look around you for other examples of ways that gravitational potential energy is converted to other forms of useful energy. One example would be falling water that turns water wheels to make mechanical energy.

CHECK IT OUT!

Read about the laws of conservation of energy. Things that are raised off the ground have gravitational potential energy. What happens to that energy when the object falls and hits the ground?

SUPER STRAW

PROBLEM

Can a straw work in a sealed bottle?

MATERIALS

drinking straw
bottle of soda
modeling clay

PROCEDURE

1. Place a straw in a bottle of soda.

2. Suck on the straw with your mouth.

3. Observe and record the results.

4. Mold a piece of clay around the straw and the mouth of the bottle. Squeeze the clay tightly around the bottle to close the opening around the straw.

5. Again suck on the straw with your mouth.

6. Observe and record the results.

RESULTS

In the open bottle, soda moves up the straw and into your mouth. The straw in the closed bottle collapses, and no liquid moves up the straw.

WHY?

Sucking on the straw removes air from the inside of the straw. In the open bottle, the air pressure outside the straw pushing down on the surface of the soda is great enough to force the liquid into the empty straw. In the closed bottle, there is not enough air to press the liquid down, so it cannot push the liquid up the straw. When the air is sucked out of the straw, the straw collapses. Air pressure is the result of gravity pulling the gas molecules in the air downward. The difference in the

inside the bottle pushing down and the force of this small amount of air is not enough to support a straw full of soda.

LET'S EXPLORE

1. To what height will air support a column of soda? Make a longer straw by attaching straws together with duct tape.

pressure of the air in the two bottles is due to the total mass of air above the surface of the liquid. In the open bottle, the column of air rises for miles (km) above the earth's surface, and the weight of this air is great **enough to hold up a straw full of soda. The closed bottle has only the trapped air**

Keep a record of the number of connected straws and the results. Be sure the connections do not leak. **Science Fair Hint:** Photographs showing the testing of the straws can be used as part of a project display.

2. Could a plastic tube replace the straw? Would it matter if the tube was not straight but coiled around?

3. Would the diameter of the straw affect the results? Repeat the experiment using fat and thin straws. **Science Fair Hint:** Display the various straws used with the results as part of a project display.

SHOW TIME!

1. How does gravity affect drinking through a straw? Would it be harder to drink through a straw on the moon than on the earth? Can astronauts drink through a straw while in an orbiting spacecraft? Display a diagram showing a person on the earth, on the moon, and in a spacecraft.

The three people are being timed as they drink soda through a straw. The amount of soda in each bottle is to indicate the ease of drinking through a straw in each environment.

2. How high is the column of air above the earth? What is the weight of the air pushing down on the soda in the open bottle? What is the total weight of the earth's atmosphere? A drawing showing a column of air above the open soda bottle with the weight and height of this column

labeled can be used as part of a project display.

CHECK IT OUT!

How does a barometer work? Why is mercury used instead of other liquids, such as water? A drawing comparing the height of a mercury barometer and a water barometer could be used as part of a project display.

16

HANGING ROCKS

PROBLEM

How does gravity affect the formation of stalactites (deposits hanging from the ceilings of caves)?

MATERIALS
distilled water
1-quart (1 liter) jar
1 tablespoon (15 ml) borax
    powder (found with
    laundry soaps in stores)
spoon
paper towel
1 teaspoon (5 ml) alum
    crystals or powder (found
    with spices in stores)

cone

PROCEDURE

1. Pour distilled water into the jar within 2 inches (5 cm) of the top.

2. Add the borax powder to the jar and stir well.

3. Fold one sheet of paper towel in half twice.

4. Place the folded corner of the towel into the jar so that the corner is about ½ inch (1.3 cm) below the surface of the liquid.

5. Pull one thickness of the paper against the top of the jar to form a paper cone.

6. Pour the alum into the cone. The alum must be in the bottom of the cone so that it touches the liquid.

7. Observe and record any changes that occur inside the jar for one hour.

RESULTS

White cloudlike particles immediately start to drift to the bottom of the jar. After about five minutes, slender structures begin to hang from the bottom of the paper cone. At the end of one hour, long,

delicate stalactite formations hang from the paper, and a mound of cloudlike material covers the bottom of the jar.

WHY?

In the bottom of the paper cone, the alum and borax combine and form a white solid called aluminum borate. Gravity pulls specks of the solid through holes in the paper towel. The downward pull of gravity on the tiny particles moves the solid through the liquid to the bottom of the jar. Some of the particles are too large to be pulled through the spaces between the paper fibers and get stuck in the openings with a portion of the particle hanging into the liquid. Other specks of the solid that fall through the holes cling to this "stuck" particle and begin the building of a formation that resembles the calcite (a mineral) deposits called **stalactites** that hang from the ceilings and sides of caves. The specks are moving slowly at the start of their descent and can easily stick to the stalactite formation. This causes the top of the structure to be larger than the bottom, and thus a wider area forms at the top, with long, slender spikes hanging down.

LET'S EXPLORE

1. Could the crystals be colored? Repeat the experiment adding a drop of red food coloring in the cone. Observe and record the movement of the color. **Science Fair Hint:** Diagrams showing the movement of the color as the stalactite forms could be used as part of a project display. Photographs of the jar would enhance the project display.

2. Does the amount of borax affect the speed of the stalactite formations? Repeat the experiment once using 2 tablespoons (30 ml) of borax and then repeat again using ½ tablespoon (7.5 ml) of borax. Record the results from the two separate experiments, and compare the results with the original experiment.

SHOW TIME!

1. How are stalactites formed in caves? Stalactites can be produced from Epsom-salt solutions. Fill two small jars

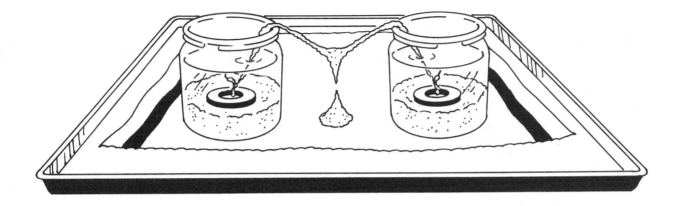

with Epsom salts. Add water to the top of the crystals in each jar and stir. Tie washers to the ends of a 12-inch (30 cm) cotton string. Place one end of the string in each of the jars. Set the jars on a tray so that they may be moved and used as part of a project display without disturbing the crystal growth. Observe for one week and make daily drawings of the crystal growth for display.

2. How are limestone stalactites and stalagmites (deposits growing up from the floors of caves) formed in nature? Pictures of natural formations could be placed on the display along with an explanation of how the crystalline structures developed. Discover the growth rate of living formations.

CHECK IT OUT!

Would stalactites and stalagmites grow in space? Discover how crystals develop in a "weightless" environment and why this is important in this age of modern technology. Write to NASA for information about space-age crystals. Your parent or teacher can assist you in securing the address.

UP AND OVER

PROBLEM

How does gravity affect the siphoning process (the movement of a liquid up and over the edge of one container and into another container at a lower level)?

MATERIALS

2 drinking glasses
water
1 flexible drinking straw

PROCEDURE

1. Fill one glass with water.

2. Bend the straw and place the short end in the glass of water.

3. Suck on the free end of the straw with your mouth until water comes out.

4. Quickly put the end of the straw into the empty glass.

RESULTS

The water flows in a steady stream up the straw then down from the higher glass to the lower glass.

WHY?

A siphon allows liquids to flow uphill. It is a device that lifts a liquid up and over the edge of one container and into another container at a lower level. To start the siphoning process, the tube must be filled with water. One way to do this is by sucking the air out of the tube. Air pressure is the result of gravity pulling gas molecules in the air downward. In the open glass, the air pressure outside the straw pushing down on the surface of the water is great enough to force the liquid up as high as the bend in the straw. Gravity then pulls the water down and out of the straw. Every drop of water that flows out of the straw leaves an empty space inside the straw. Water from the glass is pushed into the straw to fill this space. As long as the upper end of the straw remains below the surface of the water, a steady stream of liquid flows out of the lower end of the straw.

LET'S EXPLORE

1. Would the siphon work if the straw was first filled with water and placed in the glass? Fill the straw full of water; stop the ends with your fingers. Place the short end in the water of the glass sitting on the table and hold the longer end over the lower glass before removing your fingers from the ends.

2. Does it matter which end of the straw is placed in the higher glass? How high can the straw coming out of the upper glass be to keep the water flowing? Use duct tape to make straws with different heights.

3. Would the water continue to be siphoned out of the upper glass if the lower end of the straw is placed under the surface of the water in the lower container?

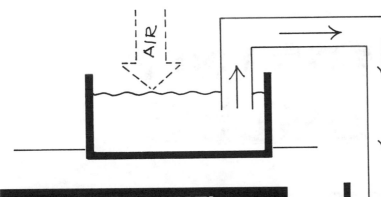

SHOW TIME!

1. What are practical uses for a siphon? Find some uses for siphons in your home, such as to transfer water out of a heavy aquarium that cannot easily be lifted. Take photographs of these examples for a project display. Point out in your oral presentation that another feature of the siphon is that liquids can be removed from the aquarium without stirring up the gravel that lies on the bottom of the tank.

2. Why does the liquid move up the shorter arm of a siphon rather than up the longer arm? Use a simple diagram similar to the one shown when explaining the movement of water through a siphon.

CHECK IT OUT!

The origin of siphons is unknown, but illustrations in Egyptian tombs provide evidence of the use of siphons as early as 1450 B.C. Read about siphons, and prepare a historical report on past and present uses. This information can be used in giving an oral presentation and/or as part of a written project report.

BLOWING BUBBLES

PROBLEM

How does gravity affect the shape of soap bubbles?

MATERIALS
¼ cup (60 ml) dishwashing
   liquid
small bowl
¼ cup (60 ml) water
spoon
1 teaspoon (5 ml) sugar
large empty thread spool

PROCEDURE
Note: This experiment should be performed outside.

1. Pour the dishwashing liquid into a small bowl.

2. Add the water to the bowl.

3. Stir the sugar into the soapy mixture to give strength to the bubbles.

4. Dip one end of the thread spool into the mixture.

5. Place your mouth against the dry end of the spool, and gently blow through the hole in the spool.

6. Blow a large bubble, and then place your finger over the hole you blew through to prevent the air from leaking out of the soap bubble.

7. Study the bubble's shape until it breaks.

8. Observe and record any movement on the surface of the bubble.

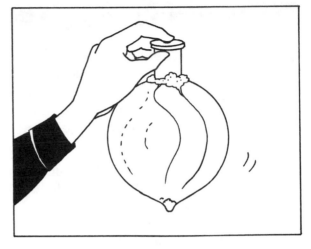

RESULTS

A bubble that is slightly pointed on the bottom hangs from the spool. Tiny, threadlike streams of liquid quickly swirl down the sides of the bubble and collect at the bottom, where they form drops and fall.

WHY?

The **molecules** (the smallest particle of the substances) of dishwashing liquid and water link together to form a thin layer of elastic liquid that stretches to surround the air blown into it. Gravity pulls the spherical bubble downward, forming a slight point at the bottom. Excess liquid on the edge of the spool is pulled down to the lowest point, collects in drops, and drips from the bottom of the bubble. The molecules that make up the thin film of the bubble are also pulled downward, causing the bubble's skin to continue to become thinner at the top until it finally breaks.

LET'S EXPLORE

1. Does the size of the bubble affect its shape? Blow a large bubble and leave the hole in the top of the spool open to allow the air to leak out. Observe and record any changes in shape as the bubble decreases in size.

2. What would be the shape of a bubble blown in a place where the gravity force is greater than on the earth? The earth's gravity (called its G-force) is given a value of one. Pulling the bubble upward quickly can simulate the results of a G-force greater than one. Blow a bubble, and hold your finger over the opening in the top of the spool. Move the spool upward, and observe any change in the shape of the bubble. Repeat using different upward speeds. **Science Fair Hint:** Record the results and make drawings of the shapes of the bubbles. Use these as part of a project display.

3. Does the shape of the opening in the spool affect the bubble's shape? Would a square or triangular hole make flat-sided bubbles and thus change the effect that gravity might have on the bubble?

SHOW TIME!

1. Photographs taken while bubbles are being blown from the different-shaped openings in the spools can be displayed along with the written results of the shape produced.

2. What shape would a soap bubble be in space? Remember that in space the pull of gravity is so weak that scientists call it **microgravity.** Everything in space is virtually weightless. Discover the shape of drops of liquids released in a spacecraft, and make drawings of the shape of bubbles in and out of a strong gravity field. Use these drawings as part of a project display.

CHECK IT OUT!

Some objects made on the earth have flaws created by the pull of gravity. How does gravity negatively affect the forming of things like marbles or ball bearings? Make a survey of materials that are difficult to make perfectly round because of gravity. Would these things be easier to make in a spacecraft?

TOYS AND GRAVITY

PROBLEM

How does gravity affect playing paddle ball?

MATERIALS
paddle ball

PROCEDURE

1. Hold the paddle in one hand and the ball in the other hand.

2. Pull the ball straight out from the paddle as far as your outstretched arms or the elastic will allow.

3. Release the ball.

4. Observe the path of the returning ball.

5. Again pull the ball straight out from the paddle as far as your outstretched arms or the elastic will allow. Raise the ball up about 1 foot (30 cm) from its horizontal position.

6. Release the ball and observe its path.

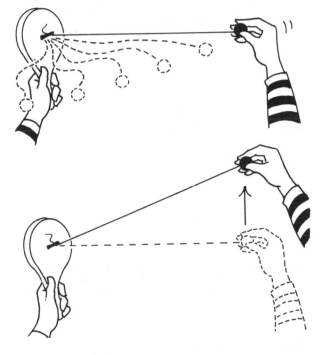

7. Continue to change the position of the ball until its returning path directs it to the center of the paddle.

RESULTS

The returning ball misses the paddle when it is stretched straight out from the paddle. Holding the ball at a height higher than the top of the paddle results in the ball striking the center of the paddle.

WHY?

The string pulls the ball toward the paddle, but gravity pulls the ball straight down. These two forces cause the ball to continue to fall and at the same time move toward the paddle. The result is that the ball moves in a curved path that arches downward. When pulled straight out, the ball's curved path brings it lower than the paddle's handle. The raised ball still moves in a curved path that arches downward, but the new path ends in the center of the paddle.

LET'S EXPLORE

How far does the ball drop before reaching the paddle? The diagram illustrates a

method for determining this distance. The paddle is partially covered with black paper and the ball dipped in flour. The ball is pulled straight out from the paddle and released. A white spot on the black paper marks the point of the returning ball. **Science Fair Hint:** The paddle and paper can be attached to the project

display and used to demonstrate the effect of gravity on the toy.

SHOW TIME!

1. Does gravity make a Slinky™ slink? Place the toy on the top step of "stairs" made by

stacking books and give it a slight push forward. Observe the movement and direction of the Slinky. Can it be made to climb up the steps? (*Note: A metal Slinky will give the best results.*) Photographs and a written description of the results can be displayed.

2. Does the height of the steps affect the movement of the Slinky? Build steps of different heights with books. Test the Slinky's movement at different heights. Display the record of each height used and the resulting movement of the toy.

3. Collect and display toys that need gravity to work. A short explanation about how each toy works with the help of gravity should accompany each toy.

CHECK IT OUT!

How would toys that depend on gravity behave in space? NASA has tested the behavior of these toys in space: paddle ball, Slinky, yo-yo, ball and jacks, flip toy, wind-up car, paper airplane. Predict and record how you think the toys might behave in space. Remember that in space the pull of gravity is so weak that objects are virtually weightless. Then find out how these toys actually behaved in space, and compare this data with your predictions. Your teacher can secure a videotape from NASA showing the actual testing of these toys during a space mission.

TALLER

How does gravity affect human height?

MATERIALS

scissors
2-liter soda bottle with cap
5 empty plastic thread
    spools
ruler
string
bowl large enough to
    support the soda bottle
helper
water

PROCEDURE

1. Have an adult use scissors to cut the bottom from a plastic soda bottle.

2. Remove any paper covering from the

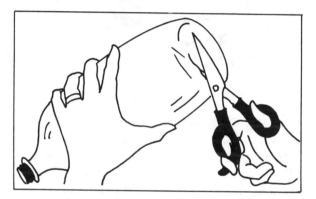

ends of the thread spools.

3. Cut an 18-inch (45 cm) length of string.

4. Place the string in the bottle with about 2 inches (5 cm) of string hanging out of the mouth of the bottle.

5. Secure the cap on the bottle, leaving part of the string hanging out.

6. Thread the free end of the string through the holes in the spools. The spools should slide down the string and stand inside the soda bottle.

7. Set the bottle, cap side down, in the large bowl.

8. Support the bottle in an upright position with your hand, and hold the upper string with your free hand so that the spools stand straight.

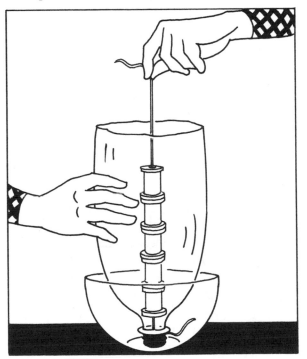

9. Compare the top of the top spool with the top of the bottle. Notice the position of each spool.

10. Ask a helper to fill the plastic bottle with water while you continue to pull the string upward.

11. Again compare the top of the top spool with the top of the bottle. Notice the position of each spool.

RESULTS
Without the water, the spools stand tightly on top of each other. When the bottle is filled with water, the spools float upward, and there is some separation between spools. The top of the top spool is lower in the empty bottle than it is in the bottle full of water.

WHY?
Without the water, gravity pulls the spools downward, causing them to stand tightly against each other. The water pushes up on the spools. This upward force by the water is called **buoyancy,** and thus the water simulates a low-gravity environment that reduces the downward pull of gravity. With less downward pull, the spools are allowed to move around more freely. They

other. In space, the discs separate, and the backbone gets longer because the body is free-falling, there is an effect of zero gravity. Astronauts in space are up to 2 inches (5 cm) taller than they are on earth!

LET'S EXPLORE

1. What effect would a different solution have on the experiment? Observe the position of the spools after each addition of 1 teaspoon (5 ml) of salt to the water. **Science Fair Hint:** This could represent the change in height with the decrease in gravity as a spacecraft moves away from the earth.

2. What would happen if the spools are connected? Cut a strip of cloth about 2 inches (5 cm) wide and 1 inch (2.5 cm) longer than the height of the stacked spools. Attach the ends of the cloth to the top and bottom spools with duct tape. Repeat the experiment. The cloth strip represents **ligaments** (a tough band of tissue connecting the ends of bones) that limit the separation of the bones in the spinal column. **Science Fair Hint:**

do not move away from each other because of the connecting string. The spinal column in the human skeletal system resembles the stack of spools in that the separate discs are free to move apart as are the spools. Like the spools, the spine has a cord; called the **spinal cord**, it runs through the centers of the discs. Gravity pulls the discs down against each

Display the spools with the attached cloth strip along with diagrams and a printed copy of the results.

SHOW TIME!

1. How does gravity affect pulse rate? One way to simulate an increase in gravity is to add weight to the body. Compare the difference in your pulse rate before and after a 2-minute walk. Carry a heavy backpack and repeat the experiment. Which walk caused the greatest increase in pulse rate? Ask volunteers to repeat the experiment, and keep records of their pulse rate before and after each walk. This information can be graphed and used as part of a project display.

2. Does your heart pump as hard as does a giraffe's? Make a heart pump as shown in the diagram. Connect straws with duct tape to equal the measurement from the top of your head to the position in which your heart lies in your chest. Squeeze the pump with your hands until the liquid in the bottle rises out of the bottle. Build a 6-foot (2 m) straw to represent a blood vessel leading from a giraffe's heart to its head. Compare the amount of effort needed to pump the liquid up both straw "blood vessels." Photographs can be used along with the actual pump and straw "vessels" as part of a project display. Prepare a written summary of the results.

CHECK IT OUT!

Astronauts discovered many changes in their bodies due to being in a "weightless" environment. Some of the changes took days, and others were apparent within minutes. Find out why the following changes occurred when there was a reduced pull of gravity on the astronauts' bodies:

- Bones lost calcium.
- Kidneys worked harder.
- There was excess fluid in the face and chest.
- Muscles shrank.
- Heart shrank.

For information, read the article called "Hang Time for Humans" in *Super Science* magazine, February 1990, Blue Edition, Scholastic Inc.

GLOSSARY

Accelerometer An instrument used to measure the pull of gravity.

Air Pressure The result of gravity pulling gas molecules in the air down toward the center of the earth.

Auxin A chemical that changes the speed of plant growth.

Balance An instrument that compares the masses of two objects.

Buoyancy The upward force exerted by a liquid such as water on any object in or on the liquid.

Center of Gravity Point at which an object balances.

Down A direction toward the earth's center.

Free-Fall The falling of an object toward the earth with no forces pulling or pushing it except gravity.

G-force Force of attraction between two objects; a G-force of one is produced by the earth's gravity.

Geosynchronous Remaining in the same position over the Earth.

Geotropism The growth of a plant due to the force of gravity.

Gravitational Attraction Force of attraction between an object and the earth, referred to as weight.

Gravitational Potential Energy Energy possessed by anything that can fall; anything raised off the ground; this energy increases with height.

Gravity A force that pulls objects on or near the earth toward its surface. The acceleration of gravity is 32 feet per second (9.8 meters per second) for every second of falling time. The direction of the pull is toward the center of the earth.

Horizontal Speed Movement parallel with a surface.

Ligament A tough band of tissue connecting the ends of bones.

Mass The amount of matter present in an object.

Microgravity A minute amount of gravitational pull; measurement of gravity in space.

Molecule The smallest particle of a substance that retains the identity of the substance.

Pendulum An object hanging from a fixed point; able to swing to and fro due to gravity and its own mass and speed.

Plumb Bob A hanging weight on a string; used by builders to show a vertical direction.

Satellite A small body moving around a larger body. The moon is a satellite of the earth.

Siphon A device that lifts a liquid up and over the edge of one container and into another container at a lower level.

Spinal Cord Cord running through the center of a vertebrate's backbone.

Spring Scale An instrument used to measure weight.

Stalactite Calcite (mineral) deposit hanging from the ceiling and sides of caves.

Stalagmite Calcite (mineral) deposit growing up from the floor of caves.

Vacuum An entirely empty space.

Viscosity Thickness of a fluid.

Weight The amount of pull that gravity has on an object.

Weightlessness Zero pull of gravity on an object; a feeling experienced by a falling object.

INDEX

**Get these fun and exciting books by Janice VanCleave
at your local bookstore, call toll-free 1-800-225-5945
or visit our Web site at: www.wiley.com/children/**

Janice VanCleave's Science for Every Kid Series
____Astronomy	53573-7	$12.95 US / 15.95 CAN
____Biology	50381-9	$11.95 US / 15.95 CAN
____Chemistry	62085-8	$11.95 US / 15.95 CAN
____Constellations	15979-4	$12.95 US / 15.95 CAN
____Dinosaurs	30812-9	$10.95 US / 15.95 CAN
____Earth Science	53010-7	$12.95 US / 15.95 CAN
____Ecology	10086-2	$10.95 US / 15.95 CAN
____Geography	59842-9	$11.95 US / 15.95 CAN
____Geometry	31141-3	$11.95 US / 15.95 CAN
____Human Body	02408-2	$12.95 US / 15.95 CAN
____Math	54265-2	$12.95 US / 15.95 CAN
____Oceans	12453-2	$12.95 US / 15.95 CAN
____Physics	52505-7	$12.95 US / 15.95 CAN

Janice VanCleave's Spectacular Science Projects Series
____Animals	55052-3	$10.95 US / 12.95 CAN
____Earthquakes	57107-5	$10.95 US / 12.95 CAN
____Electricity	31010-7	$10.95 US / 12.95 CAN
____Gravity	55050-7	$10.95 US / 12.95 CAN
____Insects & Spiders	16396-1	$10.95 US / 15.50 CAN
____Machines	57108-3	$10.95 US / 12.95 CAN
____Magnets	57106-7	$10.95 US / 12.95 CAN
____Microscopes & Magnifying Lenses	58956-X	$10.95 US / 12.95 CAN
____Molecules	55054-X	$10.95 US / 12.95 CAN
____Plants	14687-0	$10.95 US / 12.95 CAN
____Rocks & Minerals	10269-5	$10.95 US / 12.95 CAN
____Volcanoes	30811-0	$10.95 US / 12.95 CAN
____Weather	03231-X	$10.95 US / 12.95 CAN

Janice VanCleave's Science Bonanzas Series
____200 Gooey, Slippery, Slimy, Weird & Fun Experiments
	57921-1 $12.95 US / 16.95 CAN

____201 Awesome, Magical, Bizarre & Incredible Experiments
	31011-5 $12.95 US / 16.95 CAN

____202 Oozing, Bubbling, Dripping & Bouncing Experiments
	14025-2 $12.95 US / 16.95 CAN

Janice VanCleave's Guide to the Best Science Fair Projects
____Guide to the Best Science Fair Projects
	14802-4 $14.95 US / 19.95 CAN

Prices subject to change without notice.